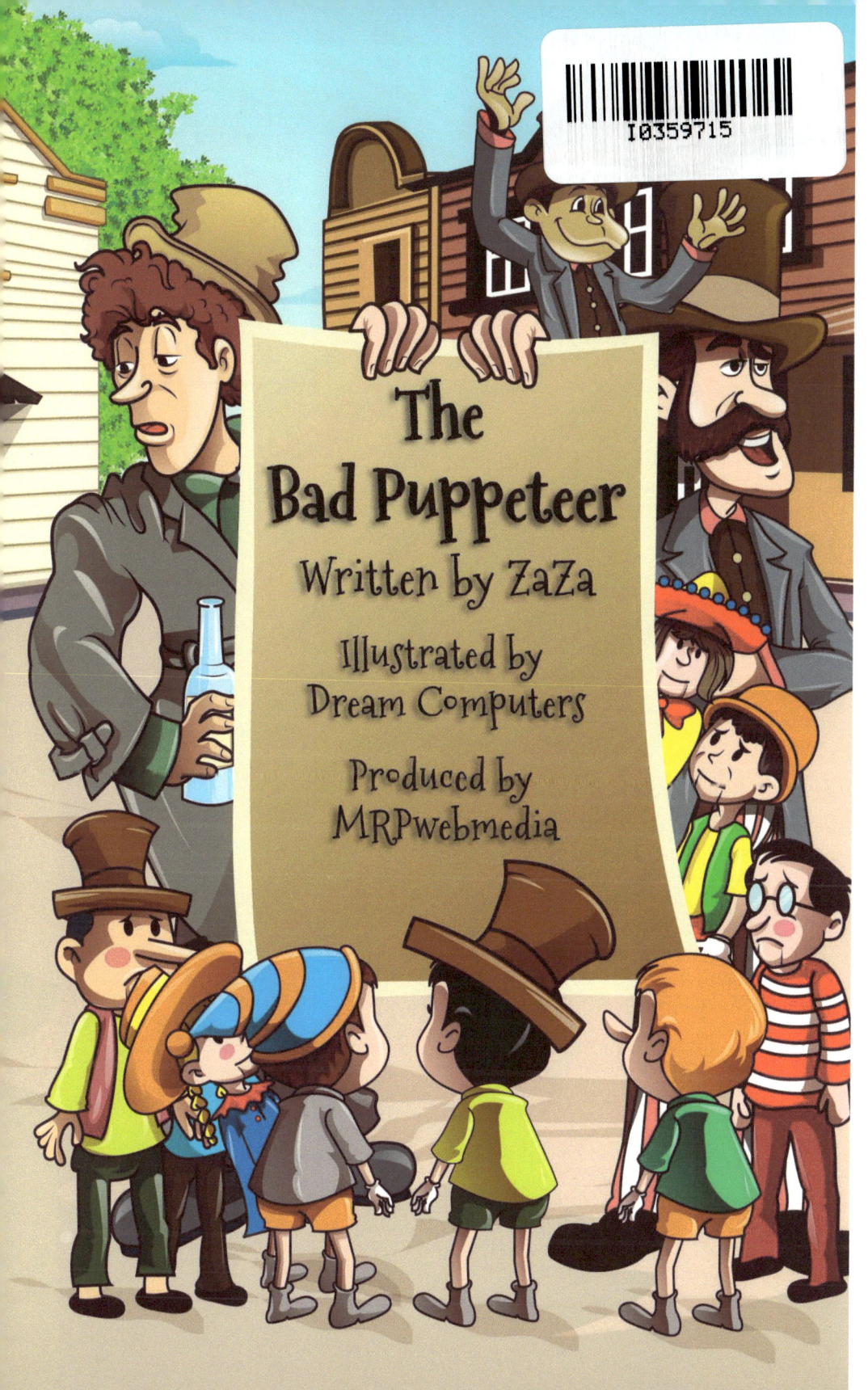

The Bad Puppeteer

Written by ZaZa
Illustrated by Dream Computers
eBook Storyteller Phil Jones
Produced by MRPwebmedia.com/books

The Bad Puppeteer

Written By ZaZa
Illustrated by Dream Computers
Produced by MRPwebmedia

ZaZa
Books for Kids

The Bad Puppeteer

Gather round people
and listen with fear,
Cause I've got a story
you've just got to hear.

It's a tale of one lonely,
sad puppeteer.
A fellow who was,
too fond of his beer.

It's a sad simple tale,
so gather all near,
For the story of one
bad puppeteer.

A fellow who was,
too fond of his cheer.

Oh there once was a sad,
a bad puppeteer,
All caused by his love,
his great love of the beer.

The puppets were angry,
the puppets were broke.
Cause their master became
such a sad silly joke.

When a performance was called,
he didn't appear,
Cause he was so fond
of his liquid foam cheer.

It's something I feel,
some don't want to hear.
The story of someone
who's too fond of beer.

The lesson to learn
seems perfectly clear,
If you want to become
a good puppeteer:

You'll have to stay clear,
stay clear of the beer.

So come one and all
for the time will grow near,
When someone will offer
a cold glass of beer.

That's the time to remember,
remember with fear
The tale of the bad,
the sad puppeteer.

So this is the story,
a sad simple tale,
Of a drunk puppeteer,
who ended in jail.

Oh there once was a sad,
a bad puppeteer,
who rotted in jail,
for his great love of the beer.

I know this is something
you don't want to hear,
The tale of the mad,
the mad puppeteer.

Now the story might be false,
it might even be true,

But whatever it is,
the moral is clear.

Stay away, stay away,
stay away from the beer,
If you ever want to become,
a good puppeteer.

The End

The Bad Puppeteer

Gather round people and listen with fear,

Cause I've got a story you've just got to hear.

It's a tale of one lonely, sad puppeteer.

A fellow who was, too fond of his beer.

It's a sad simple tale, so gather all near,

For the story of one bad puppeteer.

A fellow who was, too fond of his cheer.

Oh there once was a sad, a bad puppeteer,

All caused by his love, his great love of the beer.

The puppets were angry, the puppets were broke.

Cause their master became such a sad silly joke.

When a performance was called, he didn't appear,

Cause he was so fond of his liquid foam cheer.

It's something I feel, some don't want to hear,

The story of someone who's too fond of beer.

The lesson to learn seems perfectly clear,

If you want to become a good puppeteer:
You'll have to stay clear, stay clear of the beer.
So come one and all for the time will grow near,
When someone will offer a cold glass of beer.
That's the time to remember, remember with fear
The tale of the bad, the sad puppeteer.
So this is the story, a sad simple tale,
Of a drunk puppeteer, who ended in jail.
Oh there once was a sad, a bad puppeteer,
Who rotted in jail, for his great love of the beer.
I know this is something you don't want to hear,
The tale of the mad, the mad puppeteer.
Now the story might be false, it might even be true,
But whatever it is, the moral is clear.
Stay away, stay away, stay away from the beer,
If you ever want to become, a good puppeteer.

The End!

eBook: bit.ly/29ZhSGw
Soft Cover: amzn.to/2ay3kgP

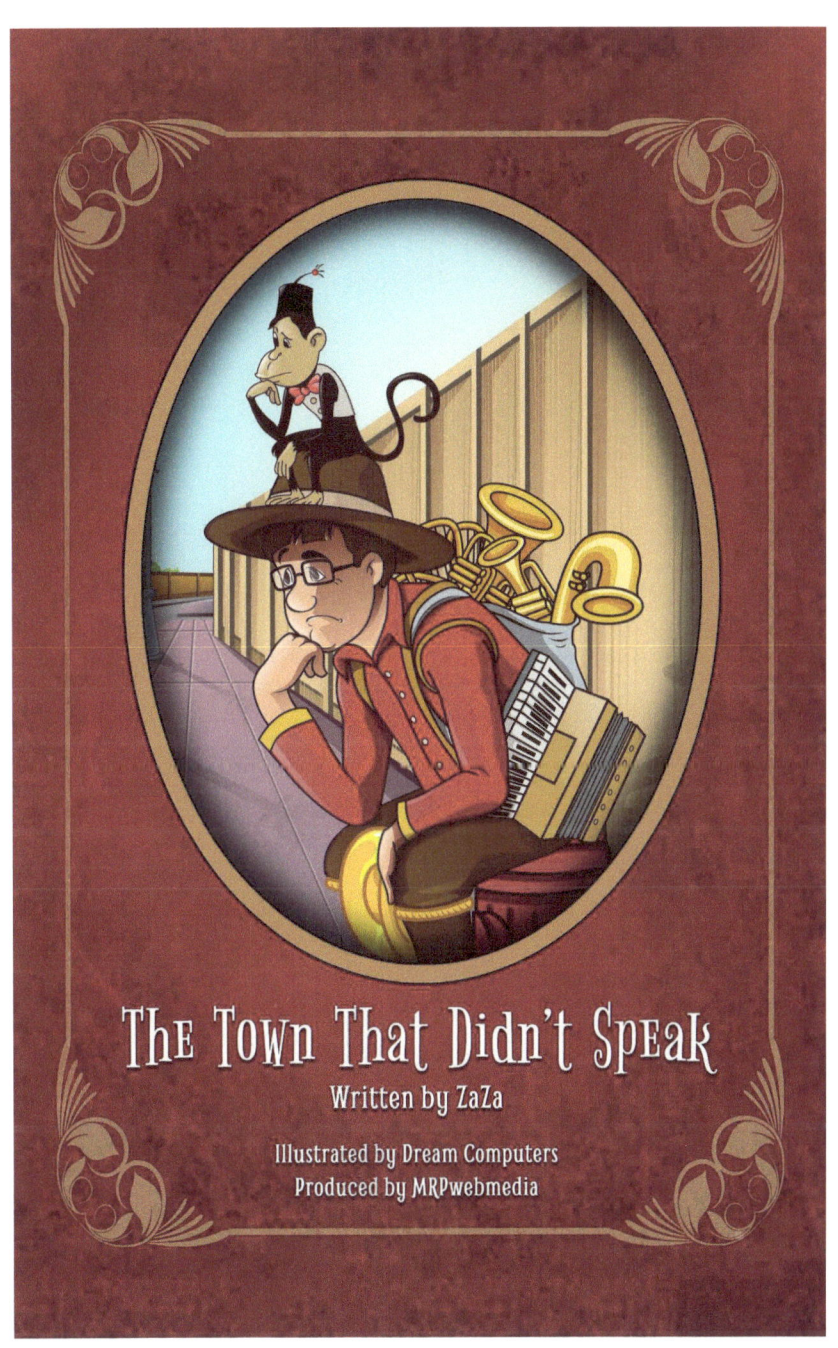

eBook: bit.ly/2dtAz8C
Soft Cover: amzn.to/2dEibKc

www.ingramcontent.com/pod-product-compliance
Lightning Source LLC
Chambersburg PA
CBHW041725070526
44586CB00001B/7